W9-CJR-284

"THE TALK"
(about money)

A Young Adult's Guide to the One Decision That Changes Everything

Dale Alexander, CFP, CLU, ChFC

STREAMLINE
BOOKS

www.WriteMyBooks.com

"THE TALK"

(about money)

A Young Adult's Guide to the ONE Decision that Changes Everything

Copyright © 2022 by Dale Alexander

All rights reserved.

No part of this book may be reproduced, distributed, or transmitted in any form or by any means, including photocopying, recording, or other electronic or mechanical methods, without the written permission from the author, except in the case of brief quotations embodied in a book review.

Cover Design by Will Severns and Chip Walters

Streamline Books

www.WriteMyBooks.com

Paperback ISBN: 979-8-8294-7049-4

Hardcover ISBN: 979-8-8294-7791-2

May 19, 2022

Contents

This senior class gift compliments of
The Georgia State Board of Education and
the Alexander Family Charitable Fund.

Congratulations! You have worked hard, persevered, and the day is finally approaching: your high-school graduation.

Now, it's time for your next step. You may be planning to enroll in a four-year university or technical college, enlist in the military, or enter the workforce. No matter which path you choose, you are entering one of the most exciting—and most important—parts of your life.

As you enter young adulthood, you'll have the opportunity and autonomy to make decisions that will impact the rest of your life. Making wise choices today can set you up for a happier, more secure, and more fulfilling tomorrow—and that includes the choices you make about money.

You may be earning your first paycheck, shifting from part- to full-time work, or taking out student loans or grants. That means it's the perfect time to strengthen your financial literacy—ensuring you have the knowledge you need to make smart decisions that will ensure a smoother path to your future dreams and goals.

I wish to thank The Alexander Family Charitable Fund for providing these materials to you, and I encourage you to review them carefully and put the knowledge you gain to action as you take on the next phase of your life. Again, I offer my sincere congratulations and wish you a successful and joyful future.

Sincerely,

Richard Woods

State School Superintendent

Georgia State Board of Education

Thanks to sponsors, no taxpayer funds were used for this project.

Disclaimer*

Now first, because investments can go down as well as go up:

The information in this book is distributed for general informational and educational purposes only and is not intended to constitute legal, tax, accounting or investment advice. All investment strategies and investments involve risk of loss. Nothing contained in this information should be construed as investment advice. Any reference to a specific investment's past or potential performance is not, and should not be construed as, a recommendation or as a guarantee of any specific outcome or profit.

Current and future investment markets may vary widely from the illustrations shown here. Past performance is no indicator of future performance.

Any ideas or strategies discussed herein should not be undertaken by any individual without prior consultation with a financial professional or counselor for the purpose of assessing whether the ideas or strategies that are discussed are suitable to you based on your own personal financial objectives, needs and risk tolerance.

Now that that's out of the way, let's get started.

Foreword

When Dale Alexander explained the big idea of this book to me, I could hardly control my excitement. While I'd acknowledge I'm a fairly passionate person, I don't say "hardly control my excitement" often. This idea captured my imagination. We nearly made a scene at the restaurant. Our volumes rose, we interrupted each other in our enthusiasm, we finished each other's sentences and ended up laughing at ourselves. I told Dale that my biggest regret about this book was that I didn't write it myself. He has captured a simple but profound idea that all of us need.

That's how strongly I feel about "The Talk" (about money).

Regardless of your age, you're about to consume some insights that will transform your life if you follow them. They will enable anyone—no matter how rich or poor they are—to shift into a higher level of lifestyle, both materially and internally. So many products and plans promise to "change your life" if you take a pill or consume a drink or follow a certain diet. Too often they ring hollow once you try them. I know Dale's ideas work because my wife and I have applied them. Or at least we've tried to for many years.

May I whet your appetite?

In this book, Dale provides you a *game plan* that could save your life. Too many Americans accidentally drift into bad habits with their money, and those bad habits permeate other areas of life. We eventually become undisciplined not only with our cash, but with our leisure time, our fitness, our clutter, our diet and our relationships. We begin reacting to situations we find ourselves in, rather than proactively working a plan so we can reach a goal. Our life looks more like we're playing "defense" rather than "offense." Once you discover and implement the "Make 70 your 100" Plan, you'll be able to live life on purpose.

As I read through the pages of this book, I found myself writing thoughts down. I encourage you to find a way to take notes as well. I found myself pausing and reflecting on how I want my adult children to discover these insights. I also scribbled down these reflections as I read:

Money is a resource. It's like a tool.

If we see ourselves as workers who have a tool to use to get a job done, we will get less emotionally attached to money and be wise as we spend it, save it, invest it or give it away. I challenge you to see money as a tool or resource to leverage in your life.

Money is a responsibility. It's like a trust.

I also believe we all will handle money better if we see it as a responsibility to manage rather than feeling like we "own" it and are entitled to be stingy with it. This enables us to become more objective about how we use it. All that we possess, we have a trust to use it well.

Money is a revealer. It's like a teller.

Finally, I believe how we handle our money is very telling about our priorities and values. It reveals where our hearts really lie. As much as we may hate to admit it, we should all examine how we spent last month's cash. It might just reveal how selfish we are.

John Wesley, the founder of the Methodist movement, put his financial philosophy this way:

• Earn all you can.

• Save all you can.

• Give all you can.

In many ways, the book in your hands compliments this philosophy. My wife and I have attempted to live this way. Over our lifetime, we've both held down jobs and had side hustles, or "gigs" on the side. We've tried to translate our talents into income. We've also tried to live by a savings plan where we automatically set income aside on a regular basis that goes into retirement savings. We don't even see it. It's set aside for the future. And for years, we've practiced planned giving to charities, non-profits and to our local church. Last year, we were able to give away twenty percent of our income. It was pure joy.

This book could be a fresh start for new habits and attitudes in your life.

As I began this foreword, I admitted I had a regret about this book. I wished I had written it myself. Thankfully, Dale has done a better job than I ever would have done. I also have a second regret. I regret that I did not learn these insights earlier in my life. I can only imagine what my career would have looked like had I practiced these truths at eighteen years old.

That's the ultimate goal.

If you get this book at the beginning of your adult life; at the launch of your career and begin to apply these ideas, you will find it easier to experience the "good life" for the rest of your time on earth. Why? You won't have to undo a bunch of bad habits. We've all heard the phrase, "All's well that ends well." Fortunately, that's true for many people. I also believe just as strongly that "All's well that begins well."

Let me encourage you. Start well. Start now. Start with you.

Tim Elmore

Founder and CEO, Growing Leaders

Introduction

Let's start with a simple question—but it's not going to be a dumb question like "Would you like to be rich?"

Nah! That's too easy. And besides, being "rich" has nothing to do with money. You can be homeless and be "rich" at the same time. Rich in lots of friends, rich in good health, happy with what you have or don't have. Content. At peace. Yeah, that's being rich!

Some of the "richest" people I've ever met live in the deepest, remote villages of inner Kenya. When I met them, it was very clear they were happy and content with what they had.

So here's the simple question:

Seeing as many Americans are broke, stressed, or anxious about their financial situation . . .

If you could have a life, where EVERY day, you'd never have to stress, worry about, be anxious over, or generally care about money, for the REST of your life, and you heard it is one of the easiest things you can ever do, would you be interested in learning how to do that?

Yes _____ No _____

If you checked "Yes," get ready!

If you checked "No," please pass this book on to someone who is, and good luck.

How we think about and use money influences the story of our lives. It reveals our values, our priorities, it makes friends and creates enemies.

It's a really weird thing, because money reveals more about ourselves than any autobiography we could ever write. I may be able to fake you into believing I like cats, but I can't fake what my checkbook reveals. Money is a scorecard for many, and is an extremely important part of our lives because money (or the lack of money) is a major cause of stress, anger, anxiety, depression and things even worse.

Many surveys show that over 50% of divorces are caused by financial stress. Financial author Howard Dayton says a more accurate marriage vow should be "Till debt do us part."

Money can be a test as well as a tool. Many people's idea of financial planning is "Spend it, then make it, THEN try and save it." Another funny saying: "Get all you can, can all you get, and sit on your can."

America, one of history's most affluent societies ever, has very few people who are able to live off the resources they have saved. Most people don't save because it involves denying something we want *now*, and the United States is not a country of *delayed* gratification. We are a country of *instant* gratification.

I guess it all boils down to this question: Do YOU OWN MONEY or does MONEY OWN YOU?

The issue is that more people are bad at handling it than are good at it. Here's one reason: money problems are not problems about money. Think about it. They are usually problems about wanting more than we can afford, greed, seeing what others have, FOMO, lack of knowledge, and other stuff like that.

I know. It's hard to even know where to begin, but it doesn't have to be. And it won't be for you.

What's the Purpose of this Book?

As you begin with Chapter 1, you'll realize this book was written for a unique purpose. While its principles will work for anyone disciplined enough to do what it says, it is specifically written for young adults . . . maybe you are about to or have recently graduated from high school or college, or even first time employees that have yet to get that first big paycheck from (what I refer to as) your FIRST, REAL job.

The reason I wrote this book is because these groups have a special, ONCE-IN-A-LIFETIME (and that is not exaggerating in the least bit) chance to change everything about not only YOUR life, but everyone that follows you. A chance to make the single greatest "life"-decision you will ever make.

I want you to have hope. I want you to understand one simple fact, and I'll repeat this throughout this little book. Here it goes:

You can be one of the wealthiest people on earth.

Is that a hard thing to grasp? Is it hard to really *believe*? I want you to know, regardless of your family's history, your own past, or even your educational background, know that this is *not* going to be hard for you to achieve.

It will, however, take a plan. Guess what? I've got that for you.

As a Certified Financial Planner® (CFP), I've always loved studying money and what to do with it. I'm always talking to my kids about money—specifically this one important principle. My kids Sophie, Grant and Davis (all young adults) and I were talking about it one night and my son Grant said, "Dad, you need to tell all our friends this story." So now you are reading what that conversation was all about. Shoutout to my kids!

By the way, every parent or guardian loves to hear their child has got a plan. So, after completing this book, you'll be able to go to them with confident statements like:

- "Hey Mom, I'm on track to be one of the wealthiest people in the country."
- "Dad, did you know the stock market is both risky AND not risky?"
- "Uncle Fred, did you know the two ways most people get wealthy are stocks and real estate?"

By the way, you will understand all of that after going through this book.

Imagine a "Future You"

For now, let's work on what YOUR FUTURE will look like.

What is your dream? We ALL have a dream. If you don't, you haven't stopped long enough to realize what it is. You should. We ALL have a vision (or at least a hope) of how we'd like our life to turn out. I'm going to make you think about it.

Because no one starts out and says, "You know, I want to get to the end of my working life and have NOTHING." No one. Certainly not you. I'm not going to let you.

This introductory exercise (which you'll read about at the end of Chapter 1) is important because not having a powerful vision of what you want leads to frustration and anger. We will fix that in the next few moments together. Here's what I know:

You will never have lasting change with anything, for a long period of time, until you have a passionate discontent combined with a powerful vision.

Or to put it in the form of a simple equation . . .

Lasting Change = a Passionate Discontent + a Powerful Vision

In the next few minutes of working through this book, I want to give you a PASSIONATE DISCONTENT. I want you to become MAD ENOUGH with BEING DISSATISFIED at how most people live their lives—which is often a constant state of worrying and being anxious about how they will make money, pay bills or ever afford to take their kids on a vacation.

Then, I want to give you a POWERFUL VISION and glimpse of what this can do to not just you (that's selfish), but everyone around and after you.

Accountability Partner(s) | Who's Your AP(s)?

I have always said that being accountable to someone is 3/4 of the completion for anything. For example, if you want to start working out and getting in shape, it is best to have someone keep you accountable. They meet you in the gym, they call you "lame" if you don't show up. Or when training for something big like a marathon, it's better if you have a *group* that you run with that holds you accountable, and a bonus if they bring big time snacks.

I want you to get a friend, or even multiple friends, and go through this workbook together. Let's call them your **Accountability Partner(s)** or **AP('s)** for short. These may be people that hold you accountable (and you hold them accountable) for what you are about to study and begin to do for the rest of your lives. So think of who you would like to go through this financial journey with. You're going to be millionaires together.

I dare you to doubt me!

Once you've talked with your **AP('s)** and committed to one another in the process, the next step is very important. Set a time that you all meet somewhere or communicate over Facetime to talk through these chapters. Some groups go through this one chapter a week, a day, etc. You do you!

You will also be cheerleaders and motivators for each other—to talk each other off the ledge when you want to buy something stupid you know you shouldn't. These **AP('s)** are a big deal, so choose wisely! The following sections in Chapter 1 are a great kick-start to read and meet with your **AP('s)** about.

As you have already seen, you'll need a pen to answer some simple true/false or yes/no questions throughout the book. Also, write any thoughts you might have in the margins of this book, because in future years it will be cool to see some of your thoughts you were having and writing out in your teens or early 20's.

One other thing: I use ALL CAPS on words I'm really passionate about. So, don't think I'm yelling at you—I'm just SUPER PASSIONATE about some of these ideas or thoughts I've seen work time and time again. And I can't wait to hear about how they work for YOU!

COME ON! LET'S GO!

See what I mean? Now let's dive into Chapter 1. Your life's about to change.

CHAPTER ONE

How Smart Are You About Money?

Okay, so let's see how smart you are about money. Get together with your **AP('s)** and let's study some interesting statements and reveal your current thoughts about money. True or False?

1. If you look rich, you probably are rich.

True _____ False _____

Answer: Your pen might have instinctively hovered to "True" but the answer is definitely FALSE! Just because someone drives a Bentley doesn't necessarily mean they're rich. There are many reasons they could have that, but not every reason means they're wealthy. They could have been given it by their parents, stolen it, rented it (like some people do when they go back home for high school reunions—you know . . . "Posers"). The person with the fancy car or giant house could also be in huge debt to pay for those things, etc. In other words, someone's look is not necessarily the same as their reality. I'll say that again:

Someone's LOOK is not necessarily the same as their REALITY.

You'd never know the average millionaire in this country, because the average millionaire really doesn't look like a millionaire. They are normal people who do normal things and make normal money. They just spend abnormally less of it than most Americans. There's a great quote that says, "People go broke trying to convince people they aren't broke."

 People go broke trying to convince people they aren't broke.

—Source Unknown

Just because you make $700,000 a year doesn't mean you are wealthy. You could only have $100,000 in the bank, and one financial hiccup and it's over. And then you could make $40,000 a year and have saved $400,000 (I've seen some of those people) and be able to retire any time you feel ready. What you make doesn't matter, it's how much less of it you spend. It's not as much the "portion" as the PRO-portion of how much you save.

In fact, someone's "look" can mean just the opposite. In their famous book *The Millionaire Next Door*, authors Thomas Stanley and William Danko say that visible symbols of wealth—cars, clothes, boats, planes and homes—are a better indicator of someone's use of *credit* than their use of money.

But as we know, social media makes their words look just like the opposite. And it's hard not to "scratch that itch" and wonder what it would be like to have those things as well. I get it—the temptation is real.

But don't be impressed by what people drive, wear, wind on their wrist or live in. The truth of the matter is that you just never know how someone got to where they are—all we can take care of and control is *our own* actions . . . and outcomes.

Alright, think hard on this next one . . .

2. "If you want to *play* on the team, go to the gym. If you want to *own* the team, go to the library."

True _____ False _____

Answer: TRUE. Who said that? Chris Gardner—the subject of the movie *The Pursuit of Happyness*, played by actor Will Smith. He was completely homeless, with a child, but worked his tail off to become a stockbroker and eventually owned his own firm. Chris and I were speaking at an event together when he told me his Momma taught him that truth. He's now reportedly worth many, many tens of millions (from what I could tell at the time of this writing). Her wisdom paid off for him, I guess.

If you want to *play* on the team, you exercise your physical talent, maybe your muscles. But if you want to *own* that team, you go to the library. You exercise your mind. What are you reading, what are you studying, because that's where you are going to have excellence. I'd rather build that up.

So, what are you building up lately? Think about what you've been reading today. Whose advice is it that you are getting educated on? Is it someone you should really be listening to, are they the success you want to be like? Do you believe they really care about you?

While we're on it, one more thing around this subject of what's going into your mind. There is a great quote by a speaker, Charlie "Tremendous" Jones that says, "You will be the same person in five years as you are today except for the people you meet (hang out with) and the books you read."

"You will be the same person in five years as you are today except for the people you meet *(or hang out with)* and the books you read."

—Charlie "Tremendous" Jones (Emphasis mine)

Who do you spend the most time with? Because the five people that are closest to you are going to determine the quality of your future. As you move forward in life, consider the people you are hanging around because they will alter the kind of life you are going to have.

Hang on. I've got to tell the truth . . . In high school, and even college, I wasn't this perfect kind of kid. But pay attention as you grow older, those relationships closest to you are going to determine the kind of life you are going to have, without a doubt. I heard a great quote about this one time . . . "If your friends don't care about their OWN future, they SURE aren't going to care about YOURS."

 "If your friends don't care about their OWN future, they SURE aren't going to care about YOURS."

—Unknown

And I challenge you to prove this next quote wrong. It is a quote from leadership expert and author John Maxwell that says, "The more you grow, the more your friends change."

 "The more you grow, the more your friends change."

—Dr. John Maxwell

You will find, as you begin addressing this greatest "life"-decision you will ever make, you will find yourself wanting to be around different type thinkers.

It's not that you are becoming stuck up or mean, or even think you are better than anyone. It is just that the higher quality of life you create, you will want to be around other high-level thinkers and doers. When you create a life of investing and giving, you will want to be around other givers and creators. But I bet this . . . you'll pull some of those people around you to even higher level lives along with you. Kind of cool to think about, isn't it? COME ON!

3. Financial success isn't buying more stuff. It's learning to live on less than you make.

True _____ False _____

Answer: TRUE. In fact, financial success is spending less than you make for a long time. Period.

Financial Success: Spend Less Than You Make for a Long Time.

That's all it takes. And the wealthy have just figured out how to have less of their money go out than comes in. Sounds like a pretty simple concept, huh? I'll show you how to do that. It really is pretty easy.

4. If I could make a lot, I would give a lot.

True _____ False _____

Answer: FALSE. I wish I could say this is true, but for many Americans (I haven't studied other countries), the more we make, the less we give.

You would think that people in general would give more, especially if they have more. But many have not learned the truth about the *paradox* of giving, which simply means it is HARDER to GIVE MORE than you GET BACK.

George Jenkins, the founder of Publix Super Markets, was once asked how much he would be worth had he NOT given away so much money. His reply was, "Probably Nothing."

George Jenkins, the founder of Publix Super Markets, was once asked how much he would be worth had he NOT given away so much money. His reply was, "Probably Nothing."

Try it. (I'm going to challenge you later.)

5. "Money makes a good person better and a bad person worse."

True _____ False _____

Answer: TRUE. Money is the great magnifier.

Do you know who said this one? Truett Cathy, the founder of Chick-fil-A.

It magnifies what is already inside us—what kind of person we really are.

If you are a taker in life, a person who only thinks about and wants more for yourself, and ends up making more money, you will use that to take more from others.

But if you are a serving type of person, if you have a giving heart, a kind spirit and end up making more money, you will use that money to do more for others and give more to others. And wow, that's when the real fun begins.

Many people have been taught that money is bad, even evil, and that people who have money are bad people who do bad things with it. In certain cases, that could be true, as it is with most everything.

But money can also solve many of the world's problems. The real question: what type of people have it and what will they do with it? My hope is for you to be blessed so that you will be a blessing to others.

My hope is for you to be blessed *so that* you will be a blessing to others.

Let's set something straight. Money is not bad. Money has no inherent qualities or traits to it. It is just a medium of exchange, how you buy and sell stuff. It's neutral. What you do with it is either good or bad. Yet it's likely that the love, or even worship, of money is a bad place to be.

My pastor at North Point Community Church in Atlanta, Andy Stanley, has a great thought about money:

 "The number one contender for our heart is our wealth."

—Andy Stanley

Money can create a tension between providing for the things we want versus solving some of the world's greatest needs. We're about to solve that tension.

But one thing I know for sure is this . . . *money is the great magnifier.*

6. Most Americans are rich.

True _____ False _____

Answer: TRUE AND FALSE. (This was a trick question).

Americans ARE wealthy from an *"international"* perspective. The amount of wealth Americans have when compared to other nations is remarkable.

If you traveled to other regions of the world and told people how you lived, many of them would find it hard to believe, that you must be from some kind of royalty. I heard once that if you ever scrape food into a garbage disposal, you are rich. If you have a pair of shoes, you are rich. If you have running water that doesn't make you sick, you're rich. Think about garages . . . our cars have their own bedrooms!!!

Think about garages . . . our cars have their own bedrooms!!!

It sounds hard to believe, but it's true. Most of the world does not live like Americans live. We are a very wealthy nation internationally. The Gallup organization did a study[1] and found that the worldwide average per capita household income is $8/day.

When people or immigrants talk about the "American Dream," a number like $8/day gives a little insight into what they mean.

Now, from a **national** perspective, we aren't doing so hot.

This is not my quote, but "the average American is a person that drives a bank-financed car over a bond-financed highway on credit card gas to open a charge account at a department store so they can fill their savings and loan-financed home with installment-purchased furniture." That's funny stuff right there. Sad, but funny.

> **"The average American is a person that drives a bank-financed car over a bond-financed highway on credit card gas to open a charge account at a department store so they can fill up their savings and loan-financed home with installment-purchased furniture."**

—Unknown

Sounds like a wonderful life, right?

I heard one man say he got a Discover Card, charged $3,000 on it and "discovered" he couldn't pay it off.

Let's look at some statistics of the average American family:

- **44% of Americans couldn't cover a $400 out-of-pocket expense.**[2]
- **Average household debt (not including the home mortgage debt) is about $38,000.**
- **In 2020, the Median US household income was $67,521.**[3]
- **Average net worth (take the value of what you own and subtract the amount you owe) is $97,000.**
- **And over half of Americans say they live paycheck-to-paycheck.**

As you can see, the average American family has little to no money saved, a large amount of monthly expenses and credit payments, and a total dependence on next month's income to stay out of bankruptcy.

In other words, we can do better. A LOT better. Let's not have you be part of these statistics, wouldn't you agree?

CHAPTER 1 EXERCISE/QUESTIONS

What is the test question you most agreed with?

_____

_____

_____

Which one surprised you most?

_____

_____

_____

Which do you doubt?

_____

_____

_____

Let's check your perspectives and attitudes about money.

1) Do you think *more highly* of people who are wealthy? (To be honest, I sometimes assume more respect for their work ethic, focus, etc., but I shouldn't because it could have come illegally or just passed down from family.)

_____

_____

_____

2) Or, are you *more critical* of people who are wealthy? If so, where does that thought come from?

_____

_____

_____

3) Do you ever think, "If only I had more money, we had a larger home, a newer car, or nicer 'stuff' then I'd be happier."? Why, or why not?

_____

_____

_____

4) As I mentioned, let's work on your future. Take a few minutes and write out what you'd like "Your Ideal Life" to look like. What industry would you like to work in, how many children would you like to have, describe your spouse, what kind of home, etc. (You'll be surprised how close to it you get).

My Ideal Life

_____

_____

_____

_____

_____

_____

_____

_____

_____

_____

_____

_____

_____

_____

_____

_____

_____

_____

CHAPTER TWO

The One Decision That Changes Everything!

Okay, here we go. This is what you came for.

If you are in high school or college, most of you reading this don't have your FIRST, REAL JOB yet. You might have a part-time job, but it's not your FIRST, REAL JOB—like one of those jobs where you fill out dental insurance forms and HR stuff from a lady named Dottie.

But at some point, you are going to go out and get that FIRST, REAL JOB. It might be driving for UPS, being a doctor, or maybe teaching.

And when you get that FIRST, REAL JOB paycheck, it will be the biggest check you will have ever gotten in your life, certainly on a regular basis. If I handed you that check today, you'd go crazy thinking about how much money you now had.

Here's the magic. I call it the "Make 70 Your 100" Plan and let me tell you, *everything* changes from here on.

When you get that FIRST, REAL JOB paycheck, instead of taking and spending all 100% of that FIRST, REAL JOB paycheck, only take 70% of it. LIVE on 70% . . . SAVE 20% . . . and GIVE 10% of it away.

Instead of spending all 100% of that FIRST, REAL JOB paycheck, only take 70% of it. LIVE on 70% . . . SAVE 20% . . . and GIVE 10% of it away.

Before you even say or think anything, it doesn't matter WHO you will give that money to. That's not important. More on that later.

Here's why this will work . . . ANY amount of FIRST, REAL JOB money is going to be higher than what you are making currently. You are basically making zero right now, compared to that FIRST, REAL JOB. You are going up! Instead of taking all 100% of that paycheck, only take 70% of it.

And listen, 70% of that FIRST, REAL JOB paycheck is still going to be the biggest paycheck you will have ever gotten in your life, at least on a regular basis. Again, if I came and gave you 70% of your FIRST, REAL JOB paycheck today, you couldn't believe how much money that would be.

70% of that FIRST, REAL JOB paycheck is STILL going to be the biggest paycheck you will have ever gotten in your life, at least on a regular basis.

This is why I say that you have a unique, ONCE-IN-A-LIFE-TIME chance (not an exaggeration) to change not only everything about YOUR life, but all of those who follow you.

"But Dale, why shouldn't I spend ALL of that money? C'mon. . . I earned it."

Listen, at your age, spending 100% of that check compared to 70% won't make a difference in your lifestyle NOW. But wait until you see what happens LATER in life because you made a decision TODAY to save that extra 30%.

Truth is, we all live on SOME percent of our paycheck . . . maybe 84%, 100%, some even 107% (ouch!). But we all try to budget and live on some percentage. You are at a once-in-a-lifetime chance to set what percent you will start living on.

Here's why this will work. My great friend, David Helton, summed up the magic formula, "You don't have a standard of living established yet. And whatever number you accept as your standard (70%), THAT becomes your reality."

 "You don't have a standard of living established yet. And whatever number you accept as your standard (70%), THAT becomes your reality."

—David Helton

I was giving "The Talk" to a school in south Georgia one day, and when I mentioned this principle, a young student up front said, "I'm going to make 50 (%) my 100%." And you know what, I believe he'll do that. He will be wealthier than he can imagine.

Again, this is still the biggest number you will have ever gotten in your life, even if you only take 70% . Make 70 your 100 (%).

Make 70 your 100 (%).

Here's some new math for you: 70 > 100.

70 > 100.

And you can do this, because remember, you are practically at $0 now, compared to the real money you will make in your career. Any new FIRST, REAL JOB money is a huge step from where you are now. That is the magic in how this can happen.

And by the way, what does the average American do? We are so cocky and arrogant about what we are going to make in the future that we not only spend 100% of that FIRST, REAL JOB check, so many of us get credit cards and blow past that and

DALE ALEXANDER, CFP, CLU, CHFC

spend about 107% of that FIRST, REAL JOB check. We think, "I've got all this money now, let's go out and load up my credit cards and buy cars and get things that I don't need with money I don't have to impress people I don't like."

But you are smarter than that. You will realize that you are going to make 70 your 100 (%), and for the rest of your life, you are going to be living inside financial margin. The other 30% will be saving 20% plus giving 10%. Life will be different for you.

Why will it be different for you?

You chose the "Make 70 Your 100" Plan . . . and you can be one of the wealthiest people on earth.

Let me address something I said earlier. I mentioned that this is the ONE "life"-decision that changes everything. Many people might say that the person you choose to marry could be the most important "life"-decision. While that is certainly important, if we don't get money right, statistically half of our marriages are gone. And out of the marriages that make it, many of them are not what they could be because of the stress and anxiety that comes with mishandling money.

You are solving that starting now with this principle of 70/20/10. And BTW, your future spouse and kids send you a hug for doing this. It's going to feel awkward . . . but just for a short time.

It's going to feel awkward . . . but just for a short time.

Let me tell you what is going to happen for a couple months after your FIRST, REAL JOB paycheck. You'll be out with some of your friends, and they will say things like,

"Hey, come on. You should buy that."

"Let's go do this."

"Why don't you spend more of your money now that you have it?!"

But you know better, because you have the "Make 70 Your 100" Plan and a purpose. And you know that the "Make 70 Your 100" Plan is far more powerful than anything you could buy today, and definitely better than the path most people your age in America are on. Nothing is better than having power and not having to use it.

But hear this! Wait for it . . .

In literally just a couple of months . . . you will be out at a restaurant with friends, and some server takes care of you very well, and you leave a $100 tip. Your friends will look at that and say, "Are you crazy!? Why would you leave that kind of tip, and how do you even do that? And what's up with these investment things like 'mutual funds' you keep talking about, what does that mean? I see you looking at investments on an app. How do you do that? Can you teach me?"

Here is why you will feel sorry for them.

This is one of the most important things in this entire book . . . pay close attention here . . .

If you take THREE (3) of those FIRST, REAL JOB paychecks, spending 100% of those checks, it will BE ALMOST IMPOSSIBLE to back down to 70%. It's over. You will have raised your expenses up to that level of income, and you will now be backed into a corner having to spend all of your money to keep up, and you will never (or highly unlikely) be able to change. And you will live life like most of America, which is broke, stressed and anxious because of the worry over money.

If you take THREE (3) of those FIRST, REAL JOB paychecks, spending 100% of those checks, it will BE ALMOST IMPOSSIBLE to back down to 70%. It's over. And you will live life like most of America, which is broke, stressed and anxious because of the worry over money.

You are THAT close to success or failure, freedom or anxiety, for the rest of your life. And it is completely in your control. But one moment in time, one decision in your life, changes everything from that day forward. It changes your grandchildrens' grandchildrens' lives. And it is this simple:

Make 70 Your 100

And you have that opportunity because it is ahead of you. I don't have that opportunity. It's behind me, it's behind your parents, and it is behind most Americans. But everyone that you know in your life who is an adult wishes they would have done what you have ahead of you to be able to do. EVERY. ONE.

If you don't believe that, take this Chapter 2 to them and let them read it. In fact, you SHOULD let them read it. They will understand the "Make 70 Your 100" Plan, then they'll get excited about it and will certainly figure out a way to make it happen. Again, every adult loves a kid with a plan—especially a plan that allows them to save and give more. In fact, if you play your cards right you might talk them into matching what you save. COME ON!!!!

If you show them this, and they say, "I wish I had done that, but it's too late for me now." Tell them this: "Not really. From now on, every new dollar that comes in, every raise you get at work, everything you sell at a garage sale, when you pay off a loan that frees up extra money, stuff like that, only take 70% of that new money."

You'll look like a hero to them. And remember . . .

You have a plan—The "Make 70 Your 100" Plan—and you can be one of the wealthiest people on earth.

Live on 70%
Save 20%
Give 10%

Or better yet: 70 > 100.

Do you agree that this is the most important "life"-decision you can make? Why or why not?

_____

_____

_____

Dale quoted David Helton—"You don't have a standard of living established yet. And whatever number you accept as your standard (70%), THAT becomes your reality."—Discuss this major point of the "Make 70 Your 100" Plan.

_____

_____

_____

"If you take THREE (3) of those FIRST, REAL JOB paychecks, spending 100% of those checks, it will BE ALMOST IMPOSSIBLE to back down to 70%. It's over."

Do you agree that you have ONE chance to get the "Make 70 Your 100" Plan right?

_____

_____

_____

(Might need a calculator for this one). If your FIRST, REAL JOB paycheck comes in at $3,500, according to the 70/20/10 principle, how much would you spend, save, and give? And what's maybe an idea of something/someone you could give that money to, and why?

_____

_____

_____

_____

_____

_____

_____

_____

_____

_____

_____

_____

_____

_____

_____

_____

CHAPTER THREE

So Prove It!

Fair enough. Here goes. Let's see what your life could look like.

Look at the "A Saving and Giving Story" chart on the following page. You're gonna have to rotate your book to get the full impact of these numbers.

Okay, that said, ready? Let's look at a great life.

A Saving and Giving Story $36,000

	1	2	3	4	5	6	7	8
	Age	Annual Salary	Monthly Salary	Monthly Spending (70%)	Monthly Savings (20%)	Yearly Investing	Investment Balance	Annual Giving 10%
Annual Raise 4.0%	23	$36,000	$3,000	$2,100	$600	$7,200	$7,470	$3,600
	24	37,440	3,120	2,184	624	7,488	15,134	3,744
Income Spent	25	38,938	3,245	2,271	649	7,788	24,443	3,894
	26	40,496	3,375	2,362	675	8,100	34,846	4,050
70%	27	42,116	3,510	2,457	702	8,424	46,448	4,212
	28	43,801	3,650	2,555	730	8,760	59,361	4,380
Income Saved	29	45,553	3,796	2,657	759	9,108	73,709	4,554
	30	47,375	3,948	2,764	790	9,480	89,624	4,740
20%	31	49,270	4,106	2,874	821	9,852	107,252	4,926
	32	51,241	4,270	2,989	854	10,248	126,751	5,124
Income Given	33	53,291	4,441	3,109	888	10,656	148,292	5,328
	34	55,423	4,619	3,233	924	11,088	172,062	5,544
10%	35	57,640	4,803	3,362	961	11,532	198,263	5,766
	36	59,946	4,996	3,497	999	11,988	227,116	5,994
Rate of Return	37	62,344	5,195	3,637	1,039	12,468	258,859	6,234
	38	64,838	5,403	3,782	1,081	12,972	293,753	6,486
8.00%	39	67,432	5,619	3,934	1,124	13,488	332,079	6,744
	40	70,129	5,844	4,091	1,169	14,028	374,144	7,014
				↓↓↓ *Fast Forward* ↓↓↓				
Age 67—Normal Social Security Retirement Age	67	$202,205	$16,850	$11,795	$3,370	$40,440	$5,229,506	$20,220
						Totals:	Savings $5,229,506	Giving $437,709

You can see this example starting at Age 23 (Column 1). That is assuming you might go on to college, or start your FIRST, REAL JOB later after high school. If you start that job sooner, your numbers could just be higher. Maybe *much* higher.

Column 2 is your Salary column. Let's assume a FIRST, REAL-JOB salary of $36,000. I use that because it's a reasonable starting income for many Americans. Starting teachers' salaries in many schools, factory workers, etc. If you think you'll make more, then your numbers will just be higher.

You will see a raise in your salary of 4% per year. That is why the salary gets higher each year. Hopefully you find a company that is doing well and passes that prosperity on to its employees.

The next Column 3 shows each of those higher annual salaries in a monthly amount. That is called your "gross" or 'total' salary each month (in this example).

The next Column 4 is where the magic happens. It shows 70% of that gross salary. In the example of a starting, yearly salary of $36,000, you will earn $3,000 per month. And 70% of that number is $2,100 per month. Instead of normal Americans (and some of your friends) taking and living on *all* of their income, your 70%, or $2,100, is going to become your 100% that you take.

As I mentioned earlier, we ALL live on some percentage of our income. It might be 70% (very few), 110%, or 100%. But we all have *some* number we try to fit our expenses inside of. Be wise and set yours way lower than your income. And this is the best time of your life to do that. You may have to live at home for one extra year, but no parent wouldn't accept that tradeoff for their kid who has a plan. Maybe a roommate for another year, cut back on the double shot Grande Macchiato EVERY day, but it's going to be worth it.

And when you approach the ripe age of 60 (which seems like a long way away, but WILL come someday), the 70% you chose to live on will pay off in MASSIVE ways.

The next column (5) shows the 20% savings, in this first year example of $3,000 monthly income X .20 (20%) = $600/month saving and/or investing. Imagine your first year of working, you are now investing $600 per month. That'd feel pretty cool, huh? Saving much more than the average American, more than most parents. And you might still be a teenager. Early 20's for sure.

Remember to stay focused,

You have a plan . . . and you can be one of the wealthiest people on earth.

Let's keep going. Column 6 shows each year, what the total yearly amount you save and invest. That goes up, remember? Because you are getting raises each year on your salary.

Column 7 shows the total saving/investing balance, adding each year, and with a rate of return on it of 8%*.

Now, the most exciting column, Column 8, the Annual Giving column. This shows each year giving 10% of the gross (or total) salary you make (and where it is given is up to you).

In the first row, you see 10% of the 36,000 salary, or $3,600 for the year. That column keeps adding all the years for the total at the bottom. Imagine your first year having to give away $300 each month. Pretty cool.

We'll talk about this later, but this Column 8 will impact your life more than any other column on this page.

Well, let's see what this looks like at the end of a career, age 67. I use that age because that is the age that full Social Security benefits* begin.

*Social Security is a retirement program that began in 1935 after the worst economic crisis in modern times, the Great Depression of 1929. The law was created to provide economic security to our nation's people. Among many things, it gives retired workers aged 62- 67 or older a continuing income after retirement. "It is the most successful anti-poverty program in our country's history." [1]

Before you even say it, "That's soooo far away." I get it. Been there, said that. The beauty of this plan is that one decision takes care of your financial life forever.

. . . one decision takes care of your financial life forever.

So, at the end, you will have GIVEN AWAY, in this example, **$437,000.** GIVEN AWAY!

And this example shows, in this scenario, accumulating **$5.2 MILLION dollars!**

Now, my financial planning classes tell me I have to disclaim this like crazy, and say things like there are no guarantees on investment returns, tax rates, raises from an employer, all sorts of stuff. I didn't guarantee any of that. I'm simply showing you numbers of a hypothetical example.*

And by the way, if you don't think you'll start at a $36,000 salary, let's start you at a $12,000 salary. See the $12,000 chart on the next page.

A Saving and Giving Story $12,000

	1	2	3	4	5	6	7	8
	Age	Annual Salary	Monthly Salary	Monthly Spending (70%)	Monthly Savings (20%)	Yearly Investing	Investment Balance	Annual Giving 10%
Annual Raise 4.0%	23	**$12,000**	1,000	700	200	2,400	2,490	1,200
	24	12,480	1,040	728	208	2,496	5,045	1,248
Income Spent 70%	25	12,979	1,082	757	216	2,592	8,148	1,296
	26	13,498	1,125	787	225	2,700	11,615	1,350
	27	14,038	1,170	819	234	2,808	15,483	1,404
	28	14,600	1,217	852	243	2,916	19,787	1,458
Income Saved 20%	29	15,184	1,265	886	253	3,036	24,569	1,518
	30	15,791	1,316	921	263	3,156	29,874	1,578
	31	16,423	1,369	958	274	3,288	35,750	1,644
	32	17,080	1,423	996	285	3,420	42,250	1,710
Income Given 10%	33	17,763	1,480	1,036	296	3,552	49,430	1,776
	34	18,474	1,540	1,078	308	3,696	57,353	1,848
	35	19,213	1,601	1,121	320	3,840	66,087	1,920
	36	19,982	1,665	1,166	333	3,996	75,704	1,998
Rate of Return 8.00%	37	20,781	1,732	1,212	346	4,152	86,285	2,076
	38	21,612	1,801	1,261	360	4,320	97,916	2,160
	39	22,476	1,873	1,311	375	4,500	110,692	2,250
	40	23,375	1,948	1,364	390	4,680	124,713	2,340
				↓↓ Fast Forward ↓↓				
Age 67-Normal Social Security Retirement Age	67	67,400	5,617	3,932	1,123	13,476	1,743,152	6,738
					Totals:		Savings $1,743,152	Giving 145,254

30

You will have still **GIVEN AWAY $145,000** and have **$1.7 MILLION dollars!** And VERY FEW people have $1.7 million dollars today.

Cool stuff huh? Getting a little better vision now? COME ON!!!

Here's a good question: do you believe this story? More importantly, do you believe it could happen TO you and FOR you?

If not, what could it be about your past that makes you think this isn't a possibility? I want you to remove those narratives—those stories that you may have heard and started to believe. Because here is a truth, NOTHING from your past must define your future. Your life is "your picture" to paint, and your canvas has an unlimited number of blessings and joys to reap.

Only YOU can see what "your picture" looks like. So go paint that bad boy!

Get with your **AP('s)** and discuss the "Life of Saving and Giving" example chart.

Do you believe it?

_____

_____

_____

What column intrigues you most, and why?

_____

_____

_____

_____

_____

CHAPTER FOUR

It's My Money.
Why Would I Give it Away?

In the "Make 70 Your 100" Plan , I mention giving 10% of your money away. Why would you ever want to do that? Well I'm glad you asked.

What is better than GETTING something for free? GIVING something for free.

 "A life can consist of two paths . . . a life built on *creating value for* or a life built on *extracting value from*."

—David Salyers, former Chick-fil-A Marketing Executive

There's no denying the fact that today, many people are suffering with loneliness, anger, depression and anxiety, not to mention suicidal thoughts. As bad as many of these issues are, we have always had that in society.

In many of these cases, hope is the ingredient that has become lost for so many of these people. That is a huge deal, because hope is the great motivator.

Hope is the great motivator.

Hope is the lift we all need that tells us there's a better path ahead —that things will get better. Doesn't that sound awesome? But there is something fighting against hope itself, something most of us never know we are battling against.

Most of what we look at (on screens) every day is built on convincing us that the way to ultimate success is by getting more for and serving ourselves. That by serving ourselves we become happiest, which is "society's pathway to success." It is what the advertising industry (through TV, social media, and print) is built on: making you dissatisfied with where you currently are. And the Industry is doing well! In fact, it is estimated that the global advertising industry will spend $1 TRILLION dollars a year by 2025. And it is aimed directly AT YOU . . . and me! And its message is the world's biggest lie. As psychologist Dr. David Schwartz says, "The ones who tell the stories define the culture."

By most of society's (social media's) standards, success is typically defined as having any of the following things: money, fame, talent or pleasure.

By most of society's (social media's) standards, being successful and happy is usually defined as having any of the following things: money, fame, talent or pleasure.

Here's the problem: when you measure success (or happiness) by society's standards, you are always left with society's outcomes. What does that mean?

You see, the world's standards of success are mostly focused on "temporary stuff". You know . . . what he's driving, how your hair looks, the beach she's laying on. But after a few hours, it's on to the next feel-good "like". And there are never enough "likes" to feed that monster. Hollywood is full of miserable rich people.

Hollywood is full of miserable rich people.

My money, it's never enough. Somebody out there has more. My talent, which eventually fades away. The cool places I go to, someone will go to cooler ones. If I have a car, it will get old and boring.

And what is feeding this unhappiness (in one of the world's wealthiest civilizations in history) is what we look at most of the day every day . . . screens. And these screens are about one thing: you're looking at Highlight Reels, and they're lying to you.

Let me prove the point.

When you see people on whatever social media platform you choose, are they happy or sad? Are they in bad places or great places? Good hair day or bad hair day? Look like they are rich or broke?

But our culture says that if you have more, if you have better, you are in some way happier and successful.

You see where this is going? Well, spoiler alert, THAT AIN'T REAL LIFE.

All you are seeing are highlight reels, and that's not the truth.

Here's an example: Have you ever seen a "GREAT" trailer for a movie, and you go see the movie and IT'S TERRIBLE. It's because all you saw were the highlight reels. And highlight reels *never* show the real story. And that is what social media is doing to us every day. Not to bash social media (I use it), but I want us to understand what it is doing to us every day. We are getting PLAYED, and by people who care nothing for us!

WHAT MATTERS MOST (in your life) matters LEAST to people that DON'T MATTER.

What matters most (in your life) matters least to people that don't matter.

For example, think about your future marriage.

What will be MOST important in your MARRIAGE, is LEAST important to Hollywood (or TV) writers and producers that want to sell the lure of a more glamorous relationship.

They don't care!

What is MOST important to your FINANCES is LEAST important to advertisers that sit around tables and talk about how to take more of your money.

They don't care about the success or impact of your life. And when we get caught in their trap, when we're unaware, we allow OUR path to be directed by those who want us to help THEIR path.

If you are lured off your path, you now walk on someone else's. And THEIR path is NOT where you want to go.

Understand . . . you are ALWAYS TRAVELING on a path.

A danger is that we see all this "stuff" they're selling us and equate a standard of living to our satisfaction with life.

Standard of Living ≠ Satisfaction with Life

They have nothing to do with each other. In fact, being in the villages of deep Kenya and seeing how happy they are with very little, I might say it's the opposite. As standard of living goes up, satisfaction with and contentment in life goes down.

It's great to be talented, or have money, or even be known. But placing our WORTH or SIGNIFICANCE in society's version of happiness brings no purpose to life. It can leave you disappointed, unhappy, and never satisfied. (Know anybody like that?)

It is killing us financially, relationally, spiritually, emotionally, on and on. Ruining us.

In *The Purpose-Driven Life*, Rick Warren says, " . . . without purpose, life has no meaning. Without meaning, life has no significance or hope." There's that word again . . . hope.

A BETTER QUESTION: What if happiness—or success—could be built on something that LASTS?

What if happiness—or success—could be built on something that "lasts"?

The greatest way to eliminate hopelessness, anxiety and despair in our lives is through serving—to consider others' best interests above our own. When you have a purpose, of serving and giving, life gets a new perspective. It is impossible to feel hopeless when you are giving hope.

It is impossible to feel hopeless when you are giving hope.

This is cool. The mind actually doesn't allow that to happen. There is something created inside each of us—dopamine, oxytocin, serotonin, endorphins—chemicals that all get released in our brains that create feelings of happiness and joy that reward you for doing good. Isn't that crazy? Our brains actually process a "reward" when we do something good for others. Like doggie treats! And what doggie doesn't like treats?

If you will build in giving 10% of your pay away each month, it will do more FOR you (and TO you) than the 20% you save and invest. Bet me on this.

If you build in giving 10% of your pay away each month, it will do more FOR you (and TO you) than the 20% you save and invest.

How can that be? It is because everyone wants to be around people that are givers. Everyone will want a piece of you if you are unselfish.

Why? Because individuals who give are rare. They are doers. They make things happen. They change lives. And you will do this without ever having to think about it. Remember . . . 70/20/10.

People will ask you to lunches for business advice—to serve on the Boards of their companies and take you places you can't imagine. You will be at donor events, meeting other successful (in the most important ways) people, showing others hope they will want to emulate. Now THAT is a highlight reel! I want so badly for your life to be a human highlight reel.

So Dale, I don't even know where to start. How do I find a place to serve, to give? How will I ever know what (or who) I should give my money to?

Answer this question: What breaks your heart?

What do you hate to see that is happening in this world, or maybe your community, and then figure out a way to use your money and talents to go solve that problem? Again, this will do far more for you than the 20% you will save and invest. I dare you to challenge me on that.

What breaks your heart?
Now go solve it.

And I hate to even say this, but the trick to this is that once you start giving 10%, that will become the most important part of your life. You won't care about the 20%. Hard to believe, isn't it?

Here's why: Wherever your heart is, your treasure will go there also.

Wherever your heart is, your treasure will go there also.

What Breaks Your Heart, and How Can You Go Solve It?

_____

_____

_____

_____

_____

_____

_____

_____

_____

_____

_____

CHAPTER 4 EXERCISE/QUESTIONS

Get your **AP('s)** together. This exercise is a little different, but fun!!!

Let's put this giving thing to the test. Challenge your **AP('s)** to save up $100 over the next few weeks. (I know that is a lot of money, but the lesson you will get from this is almost worth a college degree- and will return FAR more than $100). You might need to sell a few things online—trust me, it'll feel good to get rid of that STUFF.

Remember:

Wherever your heart is, your treasure will go there also.

Go to a restaurant. Listen to the stories the server shares with you in conversation. Before you leave, write a short and encouraging note to them. Leave a normal tip for the meal, and then under your plate leave your additional money under it with the note. Then leave.

I always like to go to a restaurant, like Waffle House, that has big windows so that I can see what is about to happen. When my family does this, usually a couple nights before Christmas, we sit outside in the parking lot and watch for the server to lift the plate and see our note with the hundred dollars.

We have seen them break down in tears, call all the other employees over to look at it, all sorts of reactions. They can't believe what has happened to them. Man, that's a cool feeling!

That is just one small example of what your entire life will be built around. Again, like we mentioned in Chapter 4, it is impossible to feel hopeless when you are giving hope.

I'd love to hear your stories of what you do with your $100. Write the experience down for your family to read in 20 years. Get ready! It's gonna' change you.

_____

_____

_____

_____

_____

_____

_____

_____

_____

_____

_____

_____

_____

_____

_____

_____

CHAPTER FIVE

_____

Why Wouldn't I Do This?

Hopefully, by Chapter 5, that's the question you're asking yourself. And it's a great question! Why would some people hear this message or read this book, and *NOT* do what I am teaching you to do? Well, there are at least four reasons I thought of:

1. Highlight Reels

The first reason is Highlight Reels, which we just covered. Again, we see the best everyone has and begin to believe we aren't good enough, rich enough, pretty enough, and on and on. That we are in some way "going backwards." Highlight Reels train us to think "I've got to keep up with so-and-so" which is also described as the Fear Of Missing Out, FOMO. That's one reason you might not apply the 70/20/10 rule.

But you just learned better. Right???

2. Stranger Danger

The next reason you might NOT do this is because of Stranger Danger (not the kind you're thinking about). This one is really interesting, and it's real! In the world of financial planning, this is a real phenomenon. I call it the "Future Self Syndrome."

Why would we NOT do things when we know they are in our best interests to do them? One of the reasons is because it could be so far into the future that we just don't care.

People know that they should save money, but that retirement thing is *way* into the future, and the future is so far off it's not really that big of an emergency for us, at least not today.

Trying to imagine ourselves 30 years into the future is as foreign to us as passing a random stranger on the sidewalk. We don't even relate to that person. To put it clearer, most people don't really care about themselves 30 years into the future . . . today.

Here's an example of that fact: Why would anyone ever smoke cigarettes? Many smokers will likely die a horribly excruciating death (but thirty years in the future). And "I really don't care about myself 30 years into the future . . . today."

The problem with that is by the time it becomes an emergency, it's too late. They say "Discipline weighs ounces. Regret weighs tons."

 "Discipline weighs ounces. Regret weighs tons."

—Jim Rohn, Motivational Speaker

But with the "Make 70 Your 100" Plan, the principle of 70/20/10% is going to automatically take care of who you are 10, 20, and 30 years from now. You will never have to worry about Future Self Syndrome from now on. You are solving it today with your plan. Done!

3. **The Boring Zone**

The next reason people may not do this is because of what I call the "Boring Zone." When you first start saving money, it is going to feel like your money is not accumulating fast, or the "Make 70 Your 100" Plan is not working at all. It could make you restless and frustrated. But you have to trust what is about to happen.

44

Look at this graph titled "The Boring Zone."

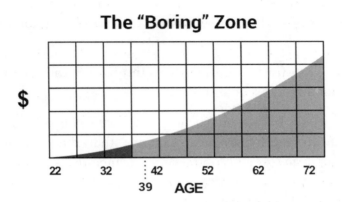

The "Boring" Zone

In the early years of your investing and saving, the money doesn't grow very much, or at least feel like it is. But you *have* to keep saving and investing. Then look at what happens after a few years. The money you keep investing, combined with the growth that is happening, will begin to compound, or build, on top of itself, and after a number of years your account should start increasing exponentially.*

This is called "Compound Interest" and we will talk about it a little later in the book.

Statistically, most of you will have eight to ten jobs in your career. Within some companies you might work for, they could have what is called a 401(k), which is a company-sponsored retirement plan that automatically takes money out of your paycheck (before taxes) and invests it. It is a great way to accumulate money (and will be part of your 20% saving amount).

But when some of you leave and go to one of those other new jobs, many people will take that money because it doesn't seem like a large amount (maybe $2,000-3,000) and spend it, instead of transferring it to the new company and putting it in the 401(k) plan there. If you keep doing that at each company you work for, that's a lot of accounts you just wasted instead of letting them add on top of each other, which can turn into *huge* amounts down the road.

You have to trust that in the future this money will start to grow and compound on top of itself.

In fact, if you look at our Saving and Giving Story example, the amount in that hypothetical example that the account grew (Column 7) at age 39 (Subtract the balance difference from age 39 to 38, $332,079 - $293,753 = $38,326) is more than the amount of salary this person started out making ($36,000).

It would be hard to believe one day, but very soon you might look at the amount that your account is earning and will not be able to believe how much it increases in a year.

To grasp this concept will place you light years ahead of the game. Just know that The Boring Zone years early on will be replaced by exciting years later.

The Boring Zone years early on will be replaced by exciting years later.

4. **Not Taught**

And the last reason some people may not do this is they have never heard this type of message. They have never been around anyone who has taught them the value of saving, investing and giving. In fact, if you know some of those people, pass this book and wisdom on to them. I, for one, thank you for passing it on. I bet they will too.

CHAPTER 5 EXERCISE/QUESTIONS

Do you believe we mostly see peoples' highlight reels on social media? Do you think it impacts you in any negative way? FOMO (Fear Of Missing Out), jealousy, envy, greed, etc.)

_____

_____

_____

Do you suffer from Stranger Danger, or putting off important things (exercise, saving, studying, etc.) because the results are far off in the future? How could you change that, if so?

_____

_____

_____

Does the Boring Zone make sense to you? How can your **AP('s)** help you stay accountable during these "Boring Zone" years?

_____

_____

_____

So What Do I Do With the 20%?

There is a difference between Saving and Investing. Saving is for short term purposes, while investing is for long term goals far into the future.

Here is the simplest way to explain it.

Short-Term Accounts

- **Checking/ATM Accounts.** These are short-term cash accounts for everyday expenses like things you need and want. There is practically no return paid on your money in return for giving you immediate access to the cash.

- **Savings Accounts**. These are for setting aside money for short-term needs to pay emergency bills or unforeseen expenses (i.e Doctor's visit for a cold, trips to see a friend, flat car tire, etc.). It is for cash that needs to be easily accessible without penalties or hassle, but accessed less often than money in an Checking/ATM Account. Financial Planners say you usually want three to six months of living expenses saved in your Savings Accounts for unexpected emergencies. This keeps you from always having to use credit cards when something goes wrong, which of course can happen in a blink. Like Checking Accounts, very little to almost no return (interest) is paid on these accounts for quick access to your money.

Your Savings Account money should not be kept in a checking account. That's too easy to get to. Also, keep it away from ATM machines if you can.

One point: This money will have very low return of interest or growth on it. That's okay. That is not what this money is for.

Long-Term Accounts

Investing is the idea of putting money away for use or enjoyment in future years. This money, historically, has had higher returns and is harder to access (have to sell your investments) and should be thought of as needed on a long-term time frame.

In this book's illustrations, I have assumed an investment return of 8%. Historically, that is less than the 10-11% return of the stock market, as measured by the S & P 500 index. Past performance is no guarantee of future results.*

If you look at the pyramid on the next page, most investments are some combination of **Cash**, **Bonds**, **Stocks** and **Real Estate**. (Don't worry, I'm about to define these in the paragraphs ahead). The lower on the pyramid, the safer the type investment it is.

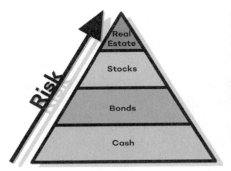

- **Cash.** In looking at this image, Cash accounts—such as checking and savings accounts at banks and credit unions, as well as money market funds—makes for the foundation of the pyramid. These accounts would be where your emergency funds are saved. This money is safe (on a day-to-day short-term basis), makes very little returns, and should be where your bills and immediate needs are paid and emergency funds are saved. Cash-type accounts mean money that is easy to access, but in the end make very little to no interest or return.

- **Bonds**. The next level in the pyramid, Bonds, can be fairly safe and are like loans to companies. Imagine you are an older person who is looking for conservative options for your money, but higher returns than say, a bank savings account. If you had $10,000, you could buy a Bond (like loaning your money to a company) that gives you a higher return, and after the length of the Bond, say 20 years, you get your money back (the Bond "maturity date"). That is all assuming the company is still in business. Bonds are normally used for more

51

conservative investors on a shorter time frame for their money. Bonds have several types of risk, such as credit risk, interest rate and opportunity risk.

- **Stocks**. Higher up the pyramid is Stocks, which means more risk is involved. Stocks are owning a piece of a company. If Bonds are "loans" then stocks are "owns". When you own a share of stock, you own a very tiny piece of a company, and the stock performance usually follows the results of the company. For example, If I bought a share of Tesla stock, then Elon Musk and I both co-own Tesla. Now, Elon owns a little bit more of it than I would. But you get the point, we are both owners in the business and if it does well, stock prices usually rise based on those results, and vice versa.

- **Real Estate**. The last level of the pyramid: Real Estate. What is that? Real estate can be comprised of homes, office buildings, condos, land, etc. Real estate can also be risky, as home and land prices do not always go up over time. Recessions or downturns in the economy could send real estate down in value, but it can also go up. The two best advantages of real estate are *Leverage* and *Rental Ability*.

The two best advantages of real estate are Leverage and Rental Ability.

Real Estate *Leverage*

Real estate "Leverage" works in the following way. Imagine you are buying a home and have $10,000 for a down payment. You buy a $100,000 home and put the $10,000 as your down payment. After some time, you decide to sell the home. Let's say the market has gone up and the home is worth $120,000. You have made $20,000, but with a down payment of only $10,000, in that example, that would actually be a 200% return. You get the Leverage on the whole value ($100,000) of the home, but a modest down payment ($10,000) for that $100,000 investment. Hard to find that in another place.

Real Estate *Rental Ability*

"Rental Ability" comes from owning that purchased home, but instead of living in it 100% of the time, you could allow others to rent it from you, effectively paying your loan (or mortgage payment) for you. So those are two great reasons for real estate as an investment, Leverage and Rental Ability. There are many other reasons also.

Realize one truth: ALL investments have risk. Cash has the risk that your money doesn't keep up with taxes and inflation. Bonds have a risk the company could go out of business. Stocks can go down, as can real estate. And there are other types of risk as well.

Having said that, the two places where more wealth is created are stocks and real estate.

The two places where more wealth is created are stocks and real estate.

Now, neither of those areas are where you are going to begin your investing. That will be in what is called a Mutual Fund.

This is big, so let's make sure you understand this. A Mutual Fund is like a bucket.

And in the bucket may be lots of stocks, lots of bonds, whatever type of investment you want to invest in. Let's use stocks, because that is most appropriate for your age and long-term time advantage.

As you begin investing, you will not have a large amount of money to spread out over many different investments to make things safer. In investing this is called diversification.

In 2020, when COVID hit the United States, many companies took a downturn in their business sales. When they did so, their stock prices plummeted as well. Do you remember entire industries like airlines and cruise line stocks and retail store stocks going down in value? At the same time, many other companies did well in sales, and consequently so did their stock prices. Golf and fitness equipment, home repair, bicycles, technology, boating, on and on. How do you make sense of it all and know where to make the right choices?

How do you make sense of it all and know where to make the right choices?

One simple answer . . . most of us don't. But the professionals do. Here's where Mutual Funds come in.

Mutual funds are huge investment funds, like a metaphorical "bucket" of money that many people invest in. And inside the bucket might be stocks of hundreds and hundreds of different companies.

What is a Mutual Fund?
...Got $25?

Amazon
Facebook
Tesla
Zoom
Clorox
Costco

Wall Street
EST. 1792

Starbucks
Apple
Google
Southwest
Delta
Carnival

*Could be hundreds of companies

The managers of your Mutual Funds are investment professionals called the "investment advisors" (that usually went to brilliant schools and have Finance and Accounting degrees), and they analyze and buy stocks and/or bonds of companies that they think are going to do well, and get rid of companies that they think are going to do poorly.

As an investor in their fund, you can buy shares, and those shares rise or fall based on how the values of the stocks in the fund perform.

The best thing about a mutual fund for the smaller investor is that we get to take advantage of their instant information, analysis and brilliant minds to do the investing and selecting FOR US and removing the stocks or bonds of the companies that they believe are not going to do well.

They have information far faster and more accurately than we have it, and are more adept and efficient at making these decisions for us.

A stock mutual fund may invest in hundreds of different companies' stocks. So it allows smaller investors with smaller dollar amounts to get great diversification (or spreading the risk) for those small dollars. Mutual funds are the best places for beginning investors to start. It doesn't guarantee safety of the main "principal" amount you invest, but makes investing for the average person much easier and better.*

So, in summary, your shorter-term money will be in things like checking and savings accounts, and your longer-term investing money will/should be in mutual funds. Those mutual funds could be individual accounts that you set up (I'll show you where to do that shortly) or in 401(K)'s offered through companies you might go work for.

CHAPTER 6 EXERCISE/QUESTIONS

Do you currently have a Checking or Savings Account, maybe at a bank or credit union?

Yes _____ No _____

Do you currently have an investment account, maybe at an investment company like Vanguard or Fidelity?

Yes _____ No _____

Discuss the concept of leverage in Real Estate and how small down payments create leverage on the total value of the piece of property you own.

_____

_____

_____

_____

_____

_____

_____

_____

_____

To begin your investment journey, I have outlined three steps to get started.

1. Get with your **AP('s)** at a coffee shop.
2. Go to TheTalkAboutMoney.com
3. Click on "Get Started" and follow the instructions to set up your first investment account.

Consider an advisor for help in selecting Investments appropriate for your situation. Before investing consider any investment objectives, risks, charges and expenses. All Investments carry some degree of risk, and past performance is no guarantee of future results. The examples used in these presentations are for illustrative purposes only and do not ensure a profit or guarantee against loss.

CHAPTER SEVEN

Is the Stock Market Risky?

What do you think? Is the Stock Market risky?

Yes _____ No _____

Answer: I would bet big money you answered "Yes." Well, either way you answered, you are correct. It's both.

Wait, I know it can be risky, but how can it be safe?

First, how can the stock market be SAFE? Let's look at the returns since 1926 of three investment types: stocks overall, bank-type savings vehicles and the 'ole cookie jar.

If we put $1 in stocks, as measured by the Ibbotson Small Company Stock Index on the next page, from 1926 that dollar would be worth over $56,000 today.[1]

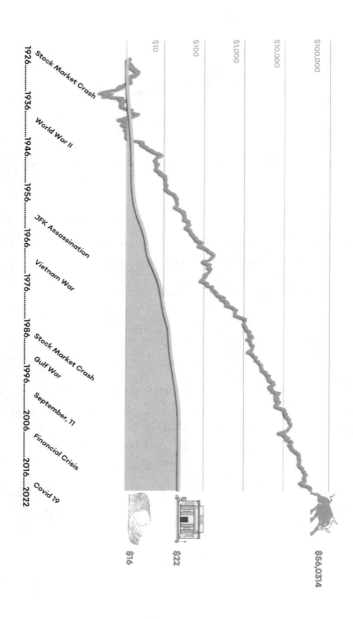

Source: Morningstar Inc. Used by permission.

But if in 1926 you invested $1 in bank-type savings vehicles, as measured by Treasury Bills, it would be worth $22 today. $22!!!!

And last, if you did nothing with it but put your dollar in a cookie jar, the $1 would need to be the equivalent of $16. Why? Because of inflation, which is the rising cost of goods over time. So your money has to do SOMETHING just to keep up with increasing prices overall, wouldn't you agree?

As an example, in 1926 the cost of a loaf of bread was five to ten cents. Today, it is around $2.

Now, in looking at this, one could infer that OVER TIME the stock market seems to be a safer place to be, right?

This is also a good time to explain that ALL investments have some type of risk, as I've stated before. You can see that what we believe to be safe investments, like bank-type investment options, OVER TIME, may turn out to not keep pace with the rising cost of goods and taxes. That is a type of risk (purchasing power risk).

ALL investments have some type of risk

On a SHORT-term basis, stocks can go down in value. That is a risk. There are many other types of risks that investments have, such as credit rating risk, international currency risk, inflation risk, and default risk among others.

"So is the stock market safe?" If investing for a long time period, then yes. It is safer than traditional fixed accounts from a LONG-term time frame.

"So is the stock market safe?" **If investing for a long time period, then yes.**

Go back to those historical returns of the stock market since 1926. Look at the bottom, X axis. If you take the worst events in world history—events where people thought the world could be over, much less their investment returns—and overlay them with the returns of the stock markets . . .you will see that most of those events barely register in the returns of the long-term growth of stocks.

"Okay, now tell me how the stock market is risky . . . "

Then is the stock market risky? Yes, it is riskier than traditional fixed accounts from a SHORT-term time frame.

As you can see on a short-term basis, year-to-year, the stock market can be down. But looking long-term at the history of it, long-term is the safer perspective to have with the stock market. So if someone needed a certain amount of money for a short-term basis, maybe five years or less, you would keep the majority of that money away from the stock market, like in your cash-type accounts.

As an example, the Arab Oil Embargo (Massive gas price increases) in the 1970's caused an economic recession that turned the stock market down for several years. If you had money for a down payment on a home, you would not have wanted that money being down in value for that long. So for short-term needs, you want money in shorter-term safe places.

Imagine the stock market like this . . . It's like yo-yoing while walking up a flight of stairs.

Imagine the stock market like this . . . It's like yo-yo-ing while walking up a flight of stairs.

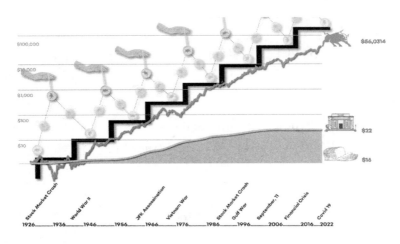

Imagine that visual, The yo-yo going up and down as you walk up a flight of stairs. From step-to-step, the yo-yo is higher and lower, but the overall flight of stairs is up. "Step-to-Step" is risky. "Floor-to-Floor", not as much. That has been the historical pattern of the stock market. Now, there are no guarantees that will continue in the future, but there are no guarantees with anything, really.*

Look back at the chart that started this chapter with just the market history alone. Do you see the ups and downs each year like a yo-yo? And do you see the long-term upward trajectory like a staircase?

In summary, from a short-term basis, the stock market is risky. But when looked at long-term, it has been safer than bank accounts and bonds. Again, that is no guarantee of the future. Just historically.*

So what does this mean for you? Next Chapter you'll find out.

CHAPTER 7 EXERCISE/QUESTIONS

Now, do you understand, and believe, that the stock market is BOTH risky AND not risky? Why and/or why not?

_____

_____

_____

What does the visual of a yo-yo going up stairs have to do with the stock market history? Is that an accurate visual of the reality of the stock market? Why or why not?

_____

_____

_____

Recap this Chapter and give your **AP('s)** an example of how you would explain to someone how the stock market is both safe AND risky.

_____

_____

_____

CHAPTER EIGHT

The Two Greatest Advantages of Being Young

In the last chapter, we saw how the stock market is safer on a long-term basis.

For example, if you needed money in a year, say for a down payment to buy a home, and consider the stock market chart from Chapter 7, you'd realize that is not the place you would save that money. From step-to-step (like the yo-yo example), we can all see the stock market is risky. But if you need this money in 30 years (floor-to-floor) it is the better place to be, right? If the stock market is the best place long-term, historically, then that lets you know that is the place you should prepare, study, and look to begin your long-term investing journey.

And here are two great reasons for doing that:

1. You have a reason to be more aggressive on the front end.
2. You have time for these investments to come back up, should markets ever go down for any period of time. And the reason those two realities work well together is because the greater the risk, typically the higher the returns.

The greater the risk, typically the higher the returns.

In more personal terms, what this allows for is the two greatest advantages you have of being young: Sale prices and warm winters. WHUT?

Hear me out . . . After a few years in the investing world, you'll notice that stocks (or your mutual funds) are one of the things people hate seeing going "on sale." Stocks "on sale" means a stock price goes down, which could also mean the money you and I have invested goes *down*. Or does it? If you aren't selling your investment, there is a difference between the "price" of an investment going down and the "value" of it going down. This is part of the beauty of being a long-term investor.

Let me explain . . .

Let's assume you want to buy some winter coats. *If you can wait*, when is the best time of the year financially to buy a winter coat? In September, at the beginning of fall or March, at the end of winter? Obviously at the end of winter when things go on sale.

Let's assume you have $100 to buy a coat, or coats, and in September coats are $100. You can only buy one coat. But in March, at the end of winter (at least in Georgia), coats go on sale for $50. So how many can I buy with my $100? Two, right?

Wait . . . are coats less valuable in the long-term? Nope.

With $100 I can now buy two coats, correct? The coat is the exact same coat. Because it went down in cost, does that mean its value has gone away? No.

Let's assume that next winter we have a warm winter and you can't wear your winter coats. Some people may be upset about that, but not you because you know that, although it's a particularly warm winter, it IS going to be cold in the future. And when it gets cold (whenever that is), you have more coats that you bought with the same amount of money. Here is what you know that many are forgetting: it will get cold again.

Dollar Cost Averaging

This act of buying more coats (stocks) when coats (stocks) go on sale is called Dollar Cost Averaging. What this means is that you continue to invest each month and if (or when) share prices go down (and you can see from the history of the stock market that happens) you continue investing, thereby automatically buying more shares (coats) when things get cheaper.

Investing is foreign territory for most people because they have wrong perspectives about it. If you don't need your investment funds for years or even decades in the future, why do you not want things going on sale periodically? Therefore, be more aggressive for a longer period of time.

Again, you're now smarter than the average bear! Let's go, Bear!

CHAPTER 8 EXERCISE/QUESTIONS

Get with your **AP('s)**. Explain the principle of Dollar Cost Averaging, and how this buys more investment shares automatically when prices go down. If needed, use the coat example Dale gave.

_____

_____

_____

Can you stay committed (long-term) when investments go down (as they always have and will)? Remember, it _will_ get cold again (and the value of those "coats" will come back).

_____

_____

_____

CHAPTER NINE

The 8th Wonder
of the World

I want to talk about what physicist Albert Einstein reportedly called the "8th Wonder of the world" and it is the principle of Compound Interest.

Simply put, Compound Interest is the money that money makes. It's not a physical object, it is simply an effect that happens on the money you will save over time.

Compound interest is the money that money makes.

And the great thing about this principle, you don't have to do a thing to get the advantages from it. Here's how Compound Interest works:

Let's assume you have $1,000 to invest. And whatever you invest that money in- say, your mutual fund- let's assume that it has a 10% rate of growth in that first year. In that example, at the end of the first year you would have $1,100, correct? We know that 10% of $1,000 is $100, so add that to your initial amount of $1,000, making $1,100.

Here's where the Compound Interest happens. LEAVE THE MONEY IN THE ACCOUNT, so that the next year's interest, or return, is multiplied, or compounded on the higher amount.

Year two, let's assume the $1,100 also earns the same rate of growth: 10%. But instead of that 10% only being $100, it is now multiplied to the full amount of $1,100, so your amount grown in the second year is now $110, or 10% of $1,100, get it? You earned $100 in the first year, and $110 in the second.

So, now you have $1,100 + 110 = $1,210.

And the amount that future interest is multiplied on gets larger and larger, and the best thing is, YOU DON'T HAVE TO DO A THING. Just leave the money alone and it happens automatically.

Money creates returns, and the returns money creates will make more returns in the long run.

Compound Interest: Money creates returns, and the returns money creates will make more returns in the long run.

Again, compound interest is not a physical thing, it is an effect on a thing: money.

Let's look at an example of this. I'll call it "The Three Employees Example."

The magic of compound interest

PAY now, PLAY later.
PLAY now, PAY later.
When you pay later, the price is always greater.

Age	Save for 9 years, then stop "Young and Smart"		Spend for 8 years, Save 35 years "Young and Dumb"		Save for 43 Years "Their Future Boss"	
	Payment	Accumulation-end of year	Payment	Accumulation-end of year	Payment	Accumulation-end of year
22	$2,000/year	$2,160			$2,000/year	$2,160
23	$2,000/year	$4,493			$2,000/year	$4,493
24	$2,000/year	$7,012			$2,000/year	$7,012
25	$2,000/year	$9,733			$2,000/year	$9,733
26	$2,000/year	$12,672			$2,000/year	$12,672
27	$2,000/year	$15,846			$2,000/year	$15,846
28	$2,000/year	$19,273			$2,000/year	$19,273
29	$2,000/year	$22,975			$2,000/year	$22,975
30	$2,000/year	$26,973		$2,158	$2,000/year	$26,973
31		$29,131	$2,000/year	$4,493	$2,000/year	$31,291
32		$31,461	$2,000/year	$7,012	$2,000/year	$35,954
33		$33,978	$2,000/year	$9,733	$2,000/year	$40,991
34		$36,697	$2,000/year	$12,672	$2,000/year	$46,430
35		$39,632	$2,000/year	$15,846	$2,000/year	$52,304
36		$42,803	$2,000/year	$19,273	$2,000/year	$58,649
↓↓↓ Fast Forward ↓↓↓						
61		$293,135	$2,000/year	$289,901	$2,000/year	$559,562
62		$316,586	$2,000/year	$315,253	$2,000/year	$606,487
63		$341,913	$2,000/year	$342,634	$2,000/year	$657,156
64		$369,266	$2,000/year	$372,204	$2,000/year	$711,899

Let's assume three employees each have $2,000/year they want to invest. The first employee (Young and Smart) puts off buying things when they start working and begins saving $2,000 per year (they **PAY** now). They save that money for 9 years and for some reason, never save another dime. When they retire, they will have accumulated $369,000 (in this example).

Instead of saving when they started work, the *second* employee (Young and Dumb) waits for those nine years (they **PLAY** now) before they began saving. In order to have approximately the same amount of money at the end of their working career, they have to save the same $2,000 per year for **EVERY YEAR** until they are 64, or 35 years!

Wait, how is that possible? (9 years investing versus 35?) The answer yet again is Compound Interest.

If you look at the row on age 31, because Employee 1 has left their money invested in the account, so that the amounts have grown, the amount of growth Employee 1 makes on their account—$2,158—is **MORE** than the $2,000 per year Employee 2 has to personally save each year. The growth is making up the payment for them.

Employee 1 built their account up fast, then let the compounding take it even faster. (**PAY NOW** so you can **PLAY LATER**).

And lastly, Employee 3 (Their Future Boss) started saving in their first year and never stopped. They *doubled* what the other two have accumulated. This is what you will do. **RIGHT?**

Oh, and by the way, the first two employees will wind up working for the third person . . . which will be you. Except you will be the **OWNER**.

It is always better to start earlier. As with most important things in your life (health, money, profession) listen to what John Maxwell says about when to start:

You can PAY NOW and PLAY LATER. Or you can PLAY NOW and PAY LATER. And when you PAY LATER, the price is always greater.

 You can PAY NOW and PLAY LATER. Or you can PLAY NOW and PAY LATER. And when you PAY LATER, the price is always greater.

—John Maxwell

So, to recap the fundamental principle of Compound Interest: Start early, LEAVE THE MONEY ALONE, and let compounding work for you.

CHAPTER 9 EXERCISE/QUESTIONS

Get with your AP('s) and discuss the first $1,000 Compound Interest example Dale used in Chapter 9.

_____

_____

_____

Then, discuss the Three Employees example. Which would you rather be? Which WILL you be?

_____

_____

_____

CHAPTER TEN

Imagine If . . .

So let me wind down the book with this . . .

This is important for your future life. Humor me with this. Call or let your **AP('s)** (Accountability Partners) know when you are going to do the following.

I want you to go somewhere quiet—a place with no distractions or interruptions. Stop reading until you are there and ready to start this exercise. When you are, turn the page and let's crank this baby up.

It's a PERFECT day . . .

Okay, imagine it is 40 years into the future. You are no longer having to work. Your family is over at your house. ALL of them. You're sitting in your backyard. (Probably in a big adirondack chair).

Maybe it's a huge backyard overlooking mountains. Maybe a marsh, a beach, or a big 'ole farm. Only you can imagine yours.

THIS DAY IS SPECIAL. You have tons of friends and family over. Some big celebration is happening. Kids are all over the place, running around and laughing. Perfect, gorgeous, sunny weather. It is a "perfect day"! The kind of day you always dreamed of.

It is a "perfect day"! The kind of day you always dreamed of.

Think about it, picture it in your mind now. Stop reading for a minute, take a sip of your Starbucks (or Dutch Bros.) and write about it.

Trust me, in 40 years, you will want to read what you will write next. I did this when I was 24, and it's almost dead on! Write out what you see this perfect day looking like.

My Perfect Day

_____

_____

_____

"THE TALK" (ABOUT MONEY)

Suddenly, one of the kids runs up to you and jumps up in your lap. It's your granddaughter. She grabs your cheeks, pulls you gently to her face, almost nose-to-nose, and says this . . . "Gan-ma (or Gan-pa), How did you do all this?"

You quickly think through the past 60 years of your life and how fast they've flown by (you even smile because you remember some guy telling you about this story—yes, that it really came true), and you tell her this:

"Well, many years ago, I got introduced to a lesson that some friends gave me. This gentleman said that if I would make '70' my '100' from the first check I ever got, he said everything about my life would change . . . my marriage would change . . . our vacations would change . . . my career, the opportunities my kids have would change. He said EVERYTHING about our life would change from that one decision. And I don't know why, but I believed what he said. So I did it. And you know what? It was true. And THAT . . . Baby Girl . . . is HOW WE HAVE ALL THIS!"

"And THAT . . . Baby Girl . . . is HOW WE HAVE ALL THIS!"

I want you to be encouraged. This story can be true . . . ABOUT YOU! But you have to go create it.

The GREATEST part of the story:

But the greatest thing about this story is that it doesn't matter about anything except this FIRST decision, on your FIRST check, on your FIRST job.

Has anyone ever told you these things?

Investment Advisor Robert G. Allen once said, "Many people assume wealth is a result of luck, connections, and inheritance. The last thing that people want to believe is the plain simple fact that wealthy people think differently."

Wealth is not some elitist, super-rare advantage or gift that only a few can have. It is also not a zero-sum game, where so many have to win and an equal number have to lose. However, only a few have it because many people listen to the naysayers of the world tell them lies and narratives to make themselves feel better about not having made their own financial success.

But you are different. You are RARE. After a speech I gave 28 years ago, a lady gave me her business card. 28 years ago. She wrote three simple words on the back . . . "You are exceptional."

 You are exceptional.

I still have that card. Why? Because she poured hope into me.

We are ALL different. We are ALL exceptional. It's just that some choose to BELIEVE it, while most don't. And if you believe it, then ACT like it. Do this ONE thing differently. And if you do, you bring along a WHOLE lot of other people with you, and make them exceptional also.

Now, strip away all those negative thoughts and comments and lies you've ever heard about money and "THE RICH" and get ready to deal with it on your own terms. You are prepared. You will use this as a starting point, and ONLY AS A STARTING POINT, and you will DO THIS.

(Please do this. Get your pen.)

Before you begin your journey, just to make sure you've gotten rid of all the negative thoughts, answer these questions about the "Make 70 Your 100" Plan:

Whether you came from a poor or rich family . . . DOES the "MAKE 70 YOUR 100" Plan CARE ABOUT THAT?

Yes _____ No _____

Whether you go/went to Ivy League colleges or never graduated . . . DOES the "MAKE 70 YOUR 100" Plan CARE ABOUT THAT??

Yes _____ No _____

Whether you are of a certain race, faith, or national origin . . . DOES the "MAKE 70 YOUR 100" Plan CARE ABOUT THAT??

Yes _____ No _____

The wealthy play the game one way, and that way is on offense. The rest of the world sits back on defense and wonders why life hits them so hard.

And because this is so easy (70/20/10), you will get over the "I can't" issue.

I love what investment guru Leon Howard said . . . "If something is too hard for people to understand, many people put it in a 'too hard box' and they don't do it. What I love about investing is that it is not an IQ sport . . . AT ALL."

Well said, Leon.

Most of the world has circumstances dictating to them what type of life they will have. How they will struggle. How they will have to live, what they will have to drive, where they will have to vacation. But for a very small group of people (who are the ones that just cared), they decide to dictate *their own* circumstances and make money work for them. You can WORK FOR YOUR MONEY, or you can have YOUR MONEY WORK FOR YOU. And when it does, life gives you all sorts of options.

Students sometimes ask me, "Why would you do this, Dale? What's in it for you?"

Well, first, writing this book and giving "The Talk" is part of the "giving" bucket of my life. Like I taught you, I can never give more than what I gain by going all over, speaking to students and young adults. Period. Not even close. It's the greatest work I have ever done in my over 30-year career.

Second, it's because I've lived this life I am showing you. It's real! You can't imagine what is waiting for you. Why would any sane person not want to go tell young adults how to do the same thing?

You know what? I think you're ready!

Now, it's up to you. TODAY, things will literally change for your family name. And you will be responsible for that. Your territory is about to expand. The seeds you plant are going to grow. Your job is to make yourself ready to handle the harvest. What will you do with this moment? Remember . . . your grandchildrens' grandchildren will live different lives because of one decision ONE of their ancestors is about to make. From THIS day forward, everything changes because . . .

You can be one of the wealthiest people on earth.

NO . . . you WILL be one of the wealthiest people on earth.

And you know what?

I'm proud of you.

A Pledge to My Future Generations

———————————

(DATE)

Today, everything changes for my life and future generations coming behind me, because *I choose* to live a life that is different.

I choose to take success into my own hands.

To not allow the world to dictate my circumstances, but to control my own destiny and future generations that follow me. It is an honor I am ready to earn.

I will be the difference-maker for future generations of my family. They will all reap lives of happiness and prosperity because of one decision in my life. This decision does not come without responsibility. Responsibility to give . . . and serve . . . and teach. I am preparing to live a life that is different . . .

A life built WITH others and FOR others.

I know it will be a most amazing ride.

Sincerely, ——————————————————

(SIGNATURE)

That's It. Now What?

I am proud of you. First of all, you've just finished another book.

Now, let's finish the work you've begun.

Grab your **AP('s)** (this is the most important exercise with your Accountability Partner)

Go to **TheTalkAboutMoney.com.**

Click on the **"Get Started"** Link. This document will take you through the steps to set up your first investment account. You will see various links to articles from Fidelity Investments and also Dave Ramsey, one of the nation's foremost investment experts.

I've linked this to Fidelity Investments, one of the largest and most widely recognized investment companies in the world. You may use any company to invest with that you like . . . Vanguard, Charles Schwab, etc. I just use Fidelity because I like their mobile app, customer experience, depth of products, etc. (By the way, I have no attachment to nor receive any compensation on anything you invest in)

I am providing these resources as a way to get you quickly into the investments you have been studying and thinking about. The longer you go from creating your first account lessens the chances you create your starting point. You will see the toll-free number to call them. Should you need help and call, tell them you are a young adult that is ready to change their life and start investing in Mutual Funds. They will love hearing that and talking to you.

DO NOT GIVE UP ON THIS. FINISH THE DRILL HERE. You are close!

If you need help, I would also consider finding a financial advisor somewhere near you that would be willing to help you set up your own account (for no fees or costs). I believe that you can do this yourself and do not need to pay an advisor just yet, but as your accounts grow and get bigger, at some point you may want to engage their services for a modest cost.

I believe in the value of advisors, but I also believe an advisor could help young people for no charge as part of the services in their work. I say that because you will become a large investor in years to come. Little fish grow into big fish, right?

Understand that investments go up, and they also go down. It is part of the laws of economics. You have been taught the value of time and market history. If you ever get nervous, call your advisor and let them help you (or re-read this book).

And some last words and thoughts (on random stuff):

1. **Keep your BODY and your MIND moving the rest of your life.** Keep working your mind through reading and your body through exercise, EVERY DAY.

SOMETHING. EVERY. DAY.

This little "life hack" gives your mind hope, which lifts your happiness.

2. **Work on growth more than goals.** When you are growing, it's amazing how much you'll accomplish. The world draws to the people that grow. And remember, the more you grow, the more your friends change. Grow to go!

3. **Start your own business one day.** Invest in yourself. This will take years. This will take sacrifice (as will working ANYWHERE). But build YOUR net worth, not somebody else's. And then you will work out of your OWN office building that you bought when you initiated the "Make 70 Your 100" Plan based on 70-20-10 (%).

Now, to make your own business work, you have to serve other people. You have to give more than they can get for what they pay. And you have to do this better than your competitors. But every customer you get is adding value to your balance sheet.

And compliment people along the way. Period.

I love you. I am so proud of you. Well done.

Oh, one other thing . . .

Write to me and tell me your thoughts, your ideas, what you are doing with your giving amounts, etc. Email me: dale@thetalkaboutmoney.com

And visit TheTalkAboutMoney.com to learn more.

I can't wait to hear from you.

GO BE GREAT!

Dale

Acknowledgements

Writing a book is one of the scariest things to do. You basically put your thoughts out there for the world to critique, people to see your grammar skills (or lack of), and a lot of other fears. But you have to punch through instead.

What helps is having a strong community, a "tribe" that rallies around you to push and motivate you. I'd first like to thank my family, my super-wife Kimberly, and our kids, Sophie, Grant and Davis, in addition to my big bro Mark and Cathy, Hunter, Lindsey and Hannah and my incredible in-laws: Lisa, Jim, Tanner, Trevor, and Nana. They always encourage me to Go Be Great. WE DID IT!!! Book Number 1. I love you guys!

Thanks a whole lot for Chip Walters' gifts of the graphics, charts and work he did on the branding. I wouldn't be here without his talents, patience, and constant motivation.

Thank you to David Helton, longtime friend who penned the quote, "You don't have a standard of living established yet. And whatever number you accept as your standard, that becomes your reality." (One of the most important truths in these readers' financial lives) Thanks David! That made this book better.

Next, my many proofreaders who put lipstick on this pig.

Then, the encouragers in my life, people like J-Bo, Danny and Joni Dukes, Susan Rubin, Michael Landry, Juli Renegar, Rhonda Swayze, Tony and Kelly Harrison, Jeff and Jacqueline Abbott, Rob and Michelle Smith, Steve and Nadine Turner, all the Bailey clan— Tim, Misti, and Macen, and Jill Newkirk. And Justin Smith, Zach Bertram, Tyler Horton and West Spence lift me continually. And I can't leave out Teddy (Theodore Corbin) Smith, my coach!

Then there's my Chick-fil-A dude Drew and lil' bro Will. You guys are great friends and coaches for me. Couldn't have done this without you. And Will, you and Alex at Streamline Books got this bad boy over the finish line. WOW, what a journey. But you made it so simple.

To my parents . . . My inspirational brother, Mark and I are lifted by the mere mention of our late parents' names. They proved that the obedience of the blessed will be rewarded by the strength and length of their legacy. We walk in the shadow of Warren and Louise Alexander's integrity and faithfulness. They showed us what love looks and sounds like, and how to love God and your children. If I can just be 1/10th of what they were . . .

And last, to you all reading these pages. I hope in some way this has brought you some sense of hope . . . and peace . . . and purpose. Again, the biggest dream I have for you is for your life to become one of giving, of serving. For you to see in the eyes of people you don't even know that in some way you make a difference. That you mattered.

We only live once. Don't get to the end and just have more cars and boats and "stuff". Again, my hope for you is that you will be blessed to be a blessing.

Well, I believe I'm done here. You are ready.

Oh, one last thing . . .

GO BE GREAT!

REFERENCES

1. How Smart Are You About Money?

1. *https://news.gallup.com/poll/166358/new-measures-global-income-gallup-world-poll.aspx*
2. https://www.debt.com/statistics/
3. https://www.census.gov/library/publications/2021/demo/p60-273.html

3. So Prove It!

1. https://www.ssa.gov/people/materials/pdfs/EN-05-10230.pdf

7. Is the Stock Market Risky?

1. *Underlying data is from the Ibbotson SBBI Yearbook, by Roger G Ibbotson and Rex Sinquefield. C2022 Precision Information LLC, dba Financial Fitness Group (FFG).*

Dale Alexander CFP, CLU, ChFC has served in the financial services industry since 1987. Originally from south Georgia, he and his wife Kimberly split time between Canton, GA and Jacksonville Beach, FL. They have three adult children, Sophie, Grant and Davis. Oh, and two pretty cool dogs, Harper and Jax.

He fell in love with the study of money early on in his career and that led him to earn the Certified Financial Planner® (CFP), Chartered Life Underwriter (CLU) and Chartered Financial Consultant (ChFC) designations.

His motivation for "The Talk" (as he is often asked) was to share the principles he has seen work in his life with young adults. He believes not only their life, but the lives of those around them will benefit greatly from the lessons contained in these pages.

Dale has been blessed to pour inspiration and motivation into others for all those years. As a well-known employee benefits broker, Dale also combines his passion for living with speaking and writing opportunities to impact others' lives and attitudes. His stages have included numerous corporations, association conferences, churches and school convocations. If you ever see Dale speak, one thing he wants to leave you with is passion.

Dale serves on the Boards of Camp Highland and Growing Leaders and has served as an Elder for North Point Ministries.